SUPPORTING CHILDREN WITH VISUAL IMPAIRMENT IN MAINSTREAM SCHOOLS
by Olga Miller

W

FRANKLIN WATTS
LONDON · NEW YORK · SYDNEY

First published in 1996 by Franklin Watts
96 Leonard Street, London EC2A 4RH

Franklin Watts Australia
14 Mars Road
Lane Cove
NSW 2066

Editor: Pamela Hopkinson

Design: Paul South and Richard Bradford

About the author

Olga Miller has been involved in the education of visually impaired children for over twenty years. Currently she is employed by RNIB and London University Institute of Education where she trains teachers to work with visually impaired children. Her recent publications include: *My Baby is Blind* , a set of videos and booklets for parents of congenitally blind children, and *One of the Family,* training materials for teachers and support assistants working with visually impaired children who have additional disabilities.

Acknowledgements

With thanks to the staff and students of Moor End High School, Huddersfield, Babington Community College, Leicester and Dorton House School, Kent who feature in photographs in this book. Thanks also to staff at RNIB Education Centre, Midlands and RNIB Education Centre, North.

The photographs on pages 37, 39, 40, 41, and 45 are from the *Eye to eye* tape slide pack produced by RNIB.
Samples of 'Moon' on page 50 were supplied by Mike McLinden, University of Birmingham.
The photograph on page 52 was provided by the Clearvision project.
Photographs on pages 18 and 68 by Gary Fry. Photographs on pages 7, 13, 15, 25, 26, 29, 30, 46, 48, 49, 53, 54, 55, 56 and 58 taken by Nigel Madhoo.
Illustrations by Iqbal Aslam.

A CIP catalogue record for this book is available from the British Library

ISBN 0 7496 1747 0

Dewey Classification 326.4

Printed in Great Britain

Contents

Foreword by Colin Low   **4**

Introduction   **5**

CHAPTER **1**   **The early years**   **6**

CHAPTER **2**   **Visual problems**   **21**

CHAPTER **3**   **Assessment of vision**   **34**

CHAPTER **4**   **Supporting the child in school**   **48**

CHAPTER **5**   **Training for independence**   **60**

References   **71**

Sources of information and help   **72**

Foreword

In the way human beings have developed, sight is arguably the most important sense. It is hardly surprising then, that most of us, confronted by the prospect of total or serious loss of sight, find it difficult to imagine how we would cope. Yet blindness, given a proper response on the part of the community, need not be a calamity. Many things for which sight is normally considered essential turn out to be capable of being done by other means.

A crucial part of society's response comes, of course, from teachers, classroom assistants and special educational needs co-ordinators in schools. Their unfamiliarity with sight problems and their difficulty in comprehending how anyone else could cope with what they could not contemplate coping with themselves can often be as much of a handicap to the children concerned as blindness or partial sight itself.

For such people, Olga Miller has demystified the subject of sight loss with this book. She explodes some of the commoner myths and explains patterns of response that might otherwise seem worrying. She underlines the importance of residual vision, leads us through the maze of assessment and introduces the different types of support available in school. In a modest compass, she presents a mass of information, but the accessible and user-friendly format means everything is easy to find.

With 20 years' experience of teaching visually impaired children and their teachers, Miller's approach is consistently practical; in talking of how to locate the toilets she notes: "In most schools they smell quite strongly"! She is also refreshingly hard-headed; she insists that we must be prepared to let go even if the child's mobility involves an element of risk and may include the odd bump and bang.

She is, too, on the side of the visually impaired child. She deals sensitively with mannerisms and sees the white cane more as a sign of independence than as a symbol of blindness. Her last word is a reference to the recent Code of Practice which reminds us that special educational provision will be most effective when those responsible take into account the ascertainable wishes of the child concerned.

Herself a professional, Miller insists that we should never be afraid to challenge a report on a child's vision, but says: "Do back up hunches with consistent observation of the child in a variety of situations." Anyone who takes this book as their guide should now be much better equipped to do this.

More and more children with a visual impairment are today being educated in mainstream schools. But visual impairment is still, fortunately, a low-incidence handicap in children. Educational professionals cannot, therefore, be expected to run across a visually impaired child all that often or to know automatically what to do when they do. It is reassuring that they now have this book to refer to.

Colin Low
Chairman, Education, Training and Employment Committee
Royal National Institute for the Blind

INTRODUCTION

The 1993 Education Act has placed increasing responsibility on mainstream schools to identify, assess and meet the needs of children with special educational needs. The Code of Practice arising out of the Act has specifically focused on the role of the Special Educational Needs Co-ordinator (SENCO). Whilst information may be readily available in some areas of special educational need, children with low incidence disabilities have until now seemed especially daunting to mainstream schools. The aim of this book is to give information to those staff working in mainstream schools who are likely to come into contact with a visually impaired child.

Typical questions asked by staff are:

- How can the child manage if she can't see the blackboard?
- How is my experience as a teacher going to help this child?
- Can the child be cured?
- Shouldn't they all be in special schools?

Not all questions and concerns about visual impairment will be answered in this book. The goal is to reduce anxiety about visual impairment in general and the needs of visually impaired children in particular.

My grateful thanks go to the many visually impaired children and families who have shared their thoughts and experiences with me. I would also like to thank my students and colleagues at London University, Institute of Education, and the Royal National Institute for the Blind

Olga Miller
1995

Blindness is rare. Very few children have no functional vision. Even the smallest amount of sight can make a major difference to a child's overall development. But, with appropriate help and intervention children who are blind from birth make successful progress. Such intervention should be as early as possible and take account of the needs of the whole family. Without adequate support congenitally blind children may continue to be significantly disadvantaged by their sensory loss.

True Story

Assan is ten years old and attends his local primary school. He is popular with his classmates and enjoys school. Unlike the rest of his class, however, Assan is blind.

How important is vision?

Sight has always played a central role in survival. The introduction of print and now information technology has meant a greater dependence on visual acuity. We have extended daylight by the introduction of artificial light and now take for granted the use of our eyes for more intense and prolonged periods of time.

In some instances we are becoming more aware of our enormous expectations. Many offices where employees spend prolonged amounts of time using visual display units now issue health and safety guidelines but most of us do not even consider what an intricate activity seeing really is. One of the most complex areas of all is the inter-relationship between the visual process and perception - our ability to interpret a three dimensional image focused on a two dimensional retina. This sophisticated ability to perceive space and form is increasingly the subject of research as scientists struggle to mimic what we so take for granted. Attempts so far have resulted in interesting creations such as virtual reality products where the brain is tricked into perceiving a space and depth which do not exist. Compared to our daily experience of sight these are still comparatively crude developments.

It would seem that although we start life with highly developed perceptual skills these skills are refined and informed by experience and a process of development. We 'learn' to see.

Vision provides us with information:

- on movement, form, depth, distance and space
- on shape, colour and texture

We use the information from our visual perception to:

- recognize objects
- copy actions
- build a visual memory
- develop spatial awareness

The challenge to learn is greater for a blind child. ▶

Vision most importantly acts as a bridge between information from our other senses. Sight unifies, co-ordinates and is informed by input from touch and hearing. Visual perception is a major area of activity for the human brain. It has been estimated that between 70 to 80 per cent of the total information the brain receives comes from the visual pathways.

Common myths

Many people believe that blindness brings with it the 'gift' of enhanced hearing or touch. This is not the case, children blind from birth or those who loose sight later in life have to learn to make greater use of other senses. This means it is all the more important for them to receive appropriate teaching and support as soon as possible. Another myth which persists is that those with low vision should be discouraged from using their sight for close work to avoid 'straining' their eyes. Children in particular need to be encouraged to use their vision to promote its development and should be helped to enhance their strategies to use it effectively.

True Story

Isabella is in her last year at secondary school. Three years ago she had an accident which damaged her eyes and left her with partial sight. Isabella intends to study banking when she leaves school. She has already practised the route to her new college both during the day and evening and now feels confident about the journey.

A much larger percentage of children have a severe visual loss but do retain some residual vision. Because these children may adopt very successful strategies to disguise any visual difficulties their needs can be easily missed. Low vision just as much as total blindness can pose threats to a child's development.

We now know that babies copy facial expressions much earlier than previously noted. Thus in the very early stages of development a baby establishes a visual dialogue with their carer. Parents of blind babies have found the seeming lack of response from their child greatly discouraging and often need help to interpret other forms of signal behaviour. Communication is a key factor in development. Severely visually impaired infants therefore suffer a major disadvantage in early interactions.

Finding out

A new baby arrives home from hospital. The baby's room and cot soon become covered with mobiles and toys. At this early stage we know the child is not ready to pick up objects so we suspend toys and shapes across the cot or above the child's head. The message we are trying to get across is that the world out there is worth exploring.

Now imagine that this new baby has very little or no sight. She cannot see the mobiles and most of all she may not be able to see the faces of her family. She cannot copy expressions or actions because she cannot see them. Friends and family feel ill at ease because this child does not 'do' the things we expect of her. She may be passive and does not seem to be interested in what is happening around her. Far from being motivated by sound as we would expect, she seems unresponsive and may become still when we speak to her.

Given appropriate stimulation this baby can be motivated to reach out into her environment and find out what is around her. If she has some residual vision she can also learn to 'look'. Her incidental learning will be limited and so parents and professionals play a more significant role in providing experiences the child can use to build confidence and motivation.

Special consideration will need to be given to ensure that the baby has access to:

- experience of a variety of movement in a secure environment - being held, rocked rhythmically.
- feeling the movement of others.
- the opportunity to listen to a variety of sounds but not sudden loud and unexpected noise or too much continuous background sound from television or radio. Voices are important. The baby may become very still when listening to a particularly interesting or important sound. This can often be misunderstood as lack of interest. Comfort has to be derived from touch and the expression in a voice rather than a face.
- the opportunity to use any residual vision. If the baby has some useful sight it is helpful to spend time observing how she responds to objects as well as people. At certain distances or angles she may well be able to see brightly coloured objects. If she does seem to have a preferred viewing distance then ensure that objects are presented within viewing range and from the appropriate angle.
- involvment in what is happening around her.

Beginning to move

One of the major threats to the explorative behaviour of severely visually impaired children is the precedence of sight over hearing in typical development. Children will reach towards an object because they see it. Hearing also acts as stimulation to reach but not until later in a child's development. There is therefore a possible delay in the blind child's contact with the environment outside themselves.

True Story

Sarah is two years old. She has no functional vision. She has just started to walk and moves around the room by holding on to pieces of furniture. Her parents are concerned because her movement seems very stiff. She also keeps her head down as she moves and often tilts it to one side. Sarah's mother is worried because Sarah looks so 'blind'.

Hearing acts as a stimulation to exploration. ▶

Although it is never going to be possible for a fully sighted adult really to simulate the experiences of a congenitally blind child, it is important to try to understand. This small experiment may help. Try to move around a familiar environment with your eyes closed, or better still wearing sleepshades, and ask a friend to observe you.

Very quickly you will feel your movement alter. Most people immediately put out their hands with fingers splayed, lower their head and move their feet further apart. Hip movement reduces and the result is a shuffling stiff gait with drooping shoulders and curved spine. This is quite natural as the body adopts a lower centre of gravity. Our speed of movement also slows. Short term these strategies make us feel more secure but long term we would risk uneven pressure on joints and possible curvature of the spine.

Because we have learnt to refine our movements by watching those of others, we have an appropriate 'movement memory' and body awareness. For a child such as Sarah, who has no useful vision, all her movements have developed from within. She has not had the opportunity to copy others. Hand-eye co-ordination has not been established. Movement which feels 'right' may lead to long term damage. These initial postural problems will be compounded as the child develops movement strategies to deal with:

- climbing up and down stairs
- running
- jumping.

The end result can be a child who is reluctant to move and has poor central body awareness. Restricted movement then leads to less and less exploration of the environment. In later years there may well be additional difficulties produced by poor muscle tone and weight problems from lack of exercise.

Unless the child has other disabilities such problems can be avoided by mobility training with input from a physiotherapist and mobility instructor. There are sometimes dilemmas when a child has some peripheral vision because it may mean they are forced to hold their head at unusual angles to make maximum use of their sight. Children may also be seeking to make better use of their hearing and again this may result in an unusual posture.

Careful observation of the child is very important. Families can be helped to work with their child on these early and vital skills. Mobility training will need to be available even if the child has good movement skills so they can develop their independence and later use public transport safely.

Developing listening skills

The development of effective listening skills can help not only a visually impaired child's independent movement and exploration of the environment but can also play a vital part in developing important memory skills. Understanding how sounds are made and where they come from helps the child build an auditory picture of her surroundings. One of the most fascinating uses of sound is 'echolocation'. Fully sighted people are often not aware of how much information can be gathered by the use of reflected sound from objects in the environment. Echolocation is the ability to use this type of sound.

Reflected sound may vary from the obvious echoes we have all heard to very subtle sound reflections. These subtle reflections help the individual to locate objects. Sonic radar makes use of sound this way as do bats and some sea creatures. This skill can be developed in severely visually impaired children and provides invaluable information to help them orientate themselves in the environment. Children will find a variety of ways of producing sounds to help them echolocate. Clicking fingers, hand clapping, mouth noises are all spontaneously used by children to generate the reflected sound necessary to echolocate.

To use their hearing effectively children will need help to:

- identify sounds
- locate a sound source
- interpret a sequence of sounds
- use reflected sound (echolocation)

Understanding and being understood

Vision when combined with our other senses gives us a whole 'picture' of an object or event. Impaired vision means that we are only able to perceive part of the 'picture'. Our other senses will help but we are still left with a fragmented or distorted idea of what is around us.

Those who loose some of their sight in later life retain a visual memory which will help them gain more information, but young children whose sight has been impaired from birth have to be helped to use their other senses to interpret more effectively the information from their environment. Sometimes information is lost or misunderstood and this may have a delaying effect on the development of language and cognition.

For some congenitally blind children language develops very rapidly but may be echoing or 'parroting' that of an adult without the child really having developed the underpinning concepts to give meaning to the language. There may also be a delayed use of pronouns as the child struggles to separate the concept of self from others. Many visually impaired children acquire excellent language skills but we must be careful not to make assumptions about their understanding.

Ian was terrified of bees. Nothing would induce him to enter a room if he heard the sound of an insect. If the classroom window was left open in the summer Ian would be rigid with fear in case a bee flew inside. Because the class teacher wanted to talk to the class about the pollination of plants she felt she should spend a little time preparing Ian for a discussion about insects. Ian has never had any sight but has always had very good language skills. The teacher assumed that Ian was frightened because he knew he could get stung by a bee and so she tried to reassure him but this really didn't seem to be his concern. She happened to have some butterfly specimens which she showed Ian so he could feel their wings. He seemed surprised they were so small. The teacher then explained they were larger than many other insects but Ian was not convinced. Bees were bigger than butterflies he said. They were enormous. Much bigger than his cat at home. The teacher asked him why he thought they were so large. They must be big he said because they make such a loud noise!

Ian knew how big his cat was because he had been able to touch and hold it. The bee was not something which adults would have thought desirable to let him touch. Ian had therefore made natural assumptions based on his available evidence which was entirely auditory.

Children with low vision may experience confusions and misunderstandings similar to Ian's. The child may only be able to see part of an object or may have little idea about incidents in the distance. Assumptions based on what may be inaccurate information will create further conceptual confusion.

It is important to make sure children with any sort of visual impairment are given sufficient opportunity to:

- **have hands-on experience of objects**
- **use other senses (such as smell or taste) to gather any additional information**
- **work in optimum visual conditions**
- **ask meaningful questions**

The importance of touch

Touch is a vital tool for information gathering. Hand-eye co-ordination is a skill teachers and parents are keen to foster.

> ## Looking, reaching and touching when integrated give us:
>
> - spatial awareness
> - specific information about an object
> - a means of checking and enhancing visual information
> - an early understanding of object permanence

Using a tactile map in a geography lesson. ▶

One of the most frustrating experiences for young children is that some things are out of reach and therefore cannot be touched. Because vision can give us information about distance and relative size we are still able to gain an accurate idea of things we cannot reach. For a severely visually impaired child getting an idea of a tree or house can be very difficult. Although touch is not restricted to hands alone we are ultimately limited by the size of our body. Visually impaired children must rely on sound or a hazy or incomplete image for additional distance or spatial information. Nevertheless, touch is a very effective means of exploring people and objects.

Touch gives information on texture, size and weight. Unlike sight, however, touch is not constant and requires efficient and systematic effort. The most obvious method of gathering tactual information is by the use of our hands but small children use their feet almost as effectively and should be encouraged to do so. All parts of the hands should be considered. Fingertips for example will be especially important for braille reading.

Sandra came into the office early with her guide dog Ben. She'd had a miserable journey to work. Not only was the train crowded but she hadn't been able to carry on with her book. When asked why, she held up a bandaged finger. She'd cut her finger opening Ben's dog food tin. No more reading for the rest of the week.

As with most areas of motor skills touch is refined from gross to fine:

- child learns to grasp objects
- child incorporates thumb and fingers into grasp
- child transfers object from hand to hand
- pincer movement develops

Most importantly the child's hand and finger movements become co-ordinated and fingers more dexterous. The physical skills of the child must be balanced by the perceptual ones. As well as holding the object the child needs to be able to gather useful information for:

- texture recognition
- shape and surface identification
- object discrimination
- object recognition

The child needs to be able to use different types of hand and finger pressure so that subtle textural variation is not lost. Those children who have some useful sight can be helped to use tactual experiences to aid their visual ones. Bold, bright colours as well as interesting textures are important. Children need to explore everyday objects made of as many different materials as possible and not be confined to the plastic favoured by toy manufacturers. 'Real' objects are much more informative than toy ones. Smell and taste are easily available to back up the information the child is gaining from touch if the object has been actually used.

Lina was going on a school trip. She was very excited because this was her first time away from home. Lots of the children were taking favourite toys. Lina surprised her mother by asking if she could take a blouse belonging to her. Lina has very little sight and her mother thought that perhaps she liked the texture of this particular material. Lina's mother agreed and said she would wash and iron the blouse. Lina was adamant she wanted it just as it was. Her mother asked why. "Because it smells like you Mum and it will remind me of home."

Touch gives information on texture, size and weight. ▶

Holding back

Sometimes visually impaired children are reluctant to use their hands to explore, or they may engage in a series of fairly random hand movements from which they derive very little information. Most disconcertingly of all they may use their hands and fingers to engage in stereotypic movements often called 'mannerisms'. To sighted adults and children 'eye poking' or 'pressing' is the most worrying of these behaviours. No doubt we find it hard to understand because we have all experienced great discomfort when even a particle of dust enters our eye. Therefore to see a child with their fist pressing hard into an eye socket makes us distinctly uneasy. The visually impaired child does not feel pain when engaged in this activity and does derive some stimulation and security. Other 'mannerisms' include hand-flapping, rocking and object 'twiddling' (where a small object is held in one hand and rotated or shaken). None of these activities are themselves indications of learning disabilities although it is true to say they become more common when visual impairment is associated with other difficulties.

For the teacher they do suggest that the child may be disengaged from their environment and thus may be restricting their range of learning opportunities. Parents may find such behaviour an embarrassment. More worryingly for the child is the fact that their strange behaviour may make them more isolated from their sighted peers.

Dealing with stereotypic behaviour relies on careful observation of the child. Children may engage in these activities for a variety of reasons and it is important to understand why. Some research (Troster et al 1990) suggests that these repetitive movements are part of normal development but in the case of visually impaired children these movements do not become integrated into later more complicated movement patterns. They are, however, more likely in some circumstances than others and may for instance be used because the child:

- is understimulated or bored (we would gaze out of the window)
- may be overstimulated or excited
- is tired
- is anxious
- is ill
- is concentrating

Children have to be helped to develop more acceptable strategies. Intervention should be as early as possible before these behaviours become too established. With older children it is possible to discuss 'mannerisms' and possible solutions as well as helping them to understand the effect their behaviour has on others.

Play and socialising

Annie is five and congenitally blind. She is happily playing with her pets. A visitor arrives and is talking to some of the children. Annie is keen to show the newcomer these pets which she has put in her pocket. The visitor holds out her hand expecting to see some toy animals. Annie very carefully lifts six cotton wool balls from her pocket. Each one has a name and Annie seems to be able to remember which one is which.

Visually impaired children need the opportunity to play but carers and teachers may need to be more actively involved in helping to provide these opportunities. We may need to accept that for a child like Annie the props used in her play do not visually resemble animals. Annie is using the play tools accessible to her and touch is the overriding factor in this particular symbolic play. Sound may be more significant also and some visually impaired children will use sound in the same way a sighted child would 'draw' a picture to illustrate a story. Play helps children to develop the social and physical skills for later life. Incidental learning also arises out of play.

Formalized game playing is a very important aspect of socialization and often poses particular difficulties for visually impaired children. Games often involve the use of shared props such as a skipping rope or footballs. They rely on advanced physical skills and tend to be located in large areas such as the school playground.

For visually impaired children play may be restricted by:

- poor mobility skills
- self stimulatory behaviour
- limited explorative behaviour
- poor play rewards from available toys or activities
- restricted opportunities to be creative
- fewer shared experiences

Karl was interested in the idea of drawing but his low level of functional vision meant that he could not always see the marks on the paper. Karl would quite often just tear up his picture in frustration. Eventually Karl's mother found some very bright paper and a thick black felt-tip pen. Karl was delighted with his new paper and pen. He was now able to draw and see enough of his picture to describe it to others.

Some games are particularly appropriate for visually impaired children and do foster participation as an equal peer. Games involving music and nursery rhymes naturally include visually impaired children because they place equal emphasis on auditory and memory skills. Access to symbolic and game play brings the child into the wider community of nursery and school. The culture of childhood is an important first step to independence. Early intervention is therefore vitally important for visually impaired children.

The visually impaired child may be excluded because they may have:

- poor hand-eye co-ordination
- difficulty following the movement of a ball or other children
- a 'misunderstanding' of the rules of the game because she cannot copy actions
- slow movement and thus be a disadvantage to the team

The family

Parents of disabled children have to cope with the same experiences as any other parent. They may be facing unemployment or the breakdown of a relationship. They may worry about the safety of their children or be concerned about their education. Increasingly they may be single parents without the support of an extended family. They may be immigrants learning to understand a different and sometimes hostile culture. Disability brings an additional agenda of its own.

Severe visual impairment is rare and blindness rarer, so very few of us actually know a visually impaired adult let alone a child. There is little chance to prepare a parent when disability is totally unexpected. Following a diagnosis of visual problems hospitals will probably feature more significantly in family life. It is likely to be in hospital, for instance, that a mother hears her baby is disabled. If this is soon after the birth she has to cope when she is at her most vulnerable. One father said that being told his son was blind was the worst moment of his life.

This is sometimes only the beginning of what becomes an emotional rollercoaster. The child might then have to undertake a series of treatments and possible surgery. Hopes may be raised and then dashed. New parents in particular may feel excluded and unskilled. Parents can feel disempowered as professionals take charge. The reverse may also be true. The condition is considered untreatable. The new mother is discharged with her visually impaired baby. Suddenly she has to confront a situation without any experience of either motherhood or disability.

Parents do develop strategies to cope. One mother described her approach when teaching her child independence skills. She was particularly conscious that she tended to overprotect her child:

"... you do do things for them. No matter what you say. With the best will in the world it is hard not to help ... I used to do things like go out of the room because I could not bear to watch her grope around for her shoes and so I would tell her I would wait for her in the kitchen until she was ready."

Parents and professionals

Parents are likely to have to meet a large number of professionals some of whom will have little idea about visual impairment. Because of the rareness of blindness, even doctors and nurses will be unlikely to have any direct experience. In many ways the effect of low vision is even less understood.

By the time their child reaches school age parents are likely to have fairly strong views about professional support. Overcoming any negative experiences parents may have had of professionals is an important part of accepting the child into the school environment. Co-ordinated professional support is important both to form the basis of early intervention by the peripatetic teachers responsible for visually impaired children but also in identifying the level and type of classroom support offered when the child reaches school age.

Cultural issues

Professionals, particularly those working in urban areas will have to deal sensitively with a wide range of cultural responses to disability. Recently a consultant paediatrician in a London hospital pointed out that in his area of London alone there were over one hundred different languages spoken and many different communities. Religion and traditional family expectations mean that it can sometimes be difficult for professionals to reach some disabled children. Children may appear in school who were previously unknown to services for visually impaired children. Home/school links are particularly important for these families.

Language can compound problems because first generation family members perhaps do not understand or speak sufficient English to discuss their child's visual needs. Expectations of the child may be low, particularly visually impaired female children who might be considered unmarriageable. The professional also has to deal with their own cultural expectations and be able to give support appropriate to the family circumstances and beliefs. It is important to accept the family view and work from their perceptions. If school and home do not communicate adequately parents can feel isolated by their child's disability or feel that their child has become part of another system and is now alien to the family.

One mother reflected on her daughter's education in a residential special school: "I felt she wasn't mine when she was at school all the time. She spoke differently to us. She spoke very nicely and pulled me up on a lot of things I said. I wasn't too keen on that. Manners were considered very important. I suppose it was a very middle class school. Uniform was very rigid ...it made her seem more of an outsider."

Professionals also have to deal with the anger and grief which parents experience when they find their child is disabled. Teachers may assume all is well and then find themselves heavily criticised for very little reason. Parents sometimes become overly concerned by small details and the professional becomes the butt of their frustration.

Parents need time and understanding. Professionals need to retain their objectivity if a true partnership is to emerge. Putting parents in touch with parent support groups where they can meet other parents of visually impaired children is often useful. Parents of older visually impaired children are particularly helpful to those with small children. One mother said when her baby was diagnosed as blind: "I just wanted desperately to see happy blind people. To know that he could grow up and have some sort of normal life."

Parents and professionals working together should aim to maximise every opportunity for visually impaired children to fulfil their potential both as a member of the family and the wider community.

It is important for professionals to work with the family. ▶

CHAPTER 2
VISUAL PROBLEMS

Vision is so important and has become so complex in humans that our eyes develop very early in gestation (around the twelfth week). The eye globe is also comparatively large (15mm at birth, 24mm fully developed) and will only increase in volume as we mature by another 3.25 times as opposed to our overall body volume which increases by about twenty times. Eyes are formed from the primitive forebrain and so are literally outposts of the brain. The early development of our eyes gives us enormous advantages. Unfortunately it also means that damage to the developing foetus may well result in damage to the eyes in particular. There is an especial risk to the eyes of babies who are born very prematurely. The growing number of babies surviving with very low birth weights and immature systems has meant that an increasing percentage of visually impaired children have additional disabilities.

How the eye sees

The eye is essentially a globe. Crudely speaking its function is to provide a mechanism for transmitting an image from the front of the eye to be focussed on the retina and then via the optic nerve to be processed in the brain. To maintain its shape and pressure the eye is filled with a viscous liquid.
It is helpful to think of the eye globe in three parts:

1. The front of the eye which contains the adaptations concerned with focusing and transmitting the light and image to the retina at the back of the eye. In this section of the eye are the cornea, pupil, iris and lens.

2. The middle section which is filled with liquid and maintains an optimum focusing shape and pressure within the globe.

A section through the eye. ▶

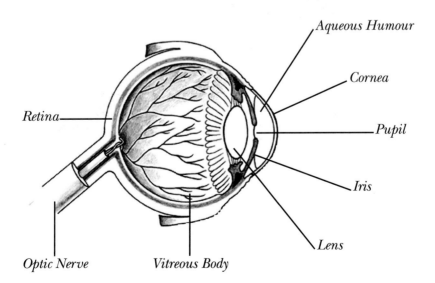

Aqueous Humour

Cornea

Retina

Pupil

Iris

Optic Nerve   Vitreous Body

Lens

21

3. The back of the eye which contains the light sensitive retina. The retina is a thin membrane made up of the cells devoted to vision. These cells are called 'rods' and 'cones'. Broadly speaking, rod cells are responsible for side vision (peripheral) in low light and cones for fine and colour vision in bright light. The area of most acute vision reception is called the 'macula'. The macula contains cone cells only.

Visual problems can be seen as:

- conditions which may lead to blindness or severe visual impairment. Even with any possible intervention either by surgery, medication or the use of lenses these conditions will still leave the child with a severe visual difficulty.
- the more common types of visual problems related to conditions associated with refractive errors or eye movements. Intervention can often be completely effective in these cases. Lenses, and training in the effective use of vision can mean that the child has minimal visual problems.
- linked with difficulties of colour discrimination and adaptation to different lighting conditions.

Transmitting nerve impulses to the brain. ▶

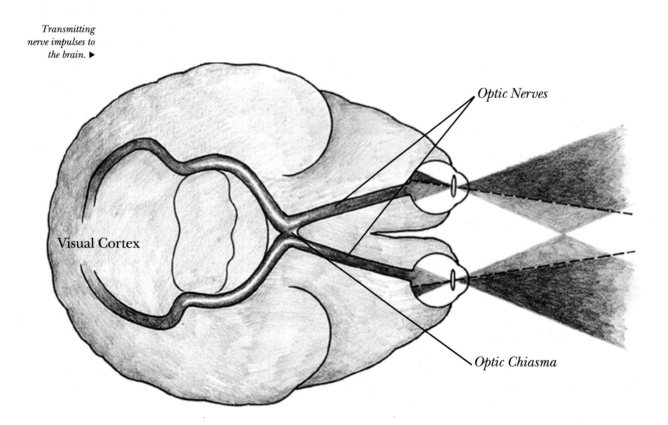

Optic Nerves

Visual Cortex

Optic Chiasma

Damage or developmental anomalies can occur to any one or a combination of the parts of the eye globe.

Our eyes are constantly moving in a series of well co-ordinated attempts to gather binocular visual information. The advantage of having two eyes is that we gain stereoscopic information and can perceive depth and distance accurately, but our eyes must work together for maximum efficiency. The co-ordinated movement of our eyes maximizes our ability to scan and track objects, people and events. Binocular information gathered from the eyes has to be transmitted to the brain. The combined input from both eyes has then to be integrated by the brain to create one image. We also need to be able to adjust the movement of our eyes and shape of our lens to bring objects into focus from far to near.

Ongoing problems may be linked with:

- a late or inaccurate diagnosis of the child's problem.
- Some visual difficulties may be 'misunderstood' as learning difficulties.

Or visual impairments may be masked by other disabilities:
- a changing and unstable visual problem
- lack of visual stimulation
- an inappropriate visual environment

Minor visual problems are common. There are very few teachers who have not come across children who need to wear glasses for some tasks at least. Many teachers are themselves spectacle wearers. Even famous clothes designers are now making spectacle frames more appealing as a fashion accessory; but it is also common for children, especially in the early years, to have undiagnosed visual problems. Even some that are diagnosed may not be remedied adequately. Assessment should take account of any possible visual problem, but what sort of eye conditions may children have? The range is enormous but from the perspective of the class teacher some are more obvious than others.

There are conditions which make the eyes look noticeably 'different', for example: squints, nystagmus, eye infections, cataracts, albinism or eye size.

Squints

There are a variety of different kinds of squint, *strabismus*. The child's eyes may seem to be looking in opposite directions or may seem to converge. Some children will have a more pronounced squint when performing a particular task. A squint may also be more noticeable if the child is tired or ill. Squints may be in one or both eyes.

But why is a squint more than a cosmetic problem? Hopefully a child who has a noticeable squint will have come to the attention of the medical profession as early as possible. This is important because good binocular vision relies on a co-ordinated set of eye movements. Children can adapt to compensate for difficulties with binocular vision but this adaptation becomes less effective as the child gets older and at the time when children's reading should be well established the child may begin to exhibit significant problems.

The main treatments for squints are glasses, patching and surgery. Some squints may be helped by the use of glasses alone. Children are likely to be still undergoing treatment for squints when they begin their nursery education but teachers should check if they think a child's eyes do not seem to be working in unison. Some squints are difficult to detect and so may well have been missed. Patching of the unaffected eye (occlusion) may be recommended in order to discourage the development of a 'lazy eye' and encourage the defective eye to work more effectively.

In the early years when a child's vision is still developing the presence of a squint can produce a confusion of visual information. In an attempt to reduce this confusion the brain will disregard information from the squinting eye. The subsequent loss of stimulation means this eye will not develop good acuity and is thus termed 'lazy' or 'amblyopic'. Even with treatment children might not develop good binocular vision. Surgery may well only have given a cosmetic benefit but it remains important for the teacher to be aware that a child has had this problem.

In class the child may:

- be clumsy, with poor hand-eye co-ordination
- have reading problems, for example, scanning difficulties
- have a general problem with tasks involving close work
- become tired or distracted during desktop activities

Nystagmus

Whilst a squint is a clear indication that a child has problematic eye movements there are also more subtle indications that a teacher may notice. Although our eyes are quite naturally constantly moving, some children may have marked differences in the rate or type of eye movement. Nystagmus is a condition in which the child's eyes may seem to oscillate. The child cannot control this movement. This condition is sometimes referred to as 'dancing eyes'. Although the child may have nystagmus without any additional eye conditions it is more common to find nystagmus associated with other focusing difficulties including squints. The child may have glasses prescribed for additional refractive errors such as short sight but glasses will not prevent the nystagmus.

The teacher will need to:
- make sure that the child has had a vision screening (see Chapter 3). Nystagmus can be a sign of other more serious conditions. At the very least, vision screening will help to remedy any refractive errors.
- notice how the child prefers to sit when 'looking' at their work. Although the child will not be conscious of the movement of their eyes they will seek to gain the clearest image. Many children will hold their heads to find the 'null' point in the nystagmus. This is the point at which the nystagmus is reduced and the child's vision is at its clearest. Some children may need help to find this 'null' position.
- encourage the child to choose optimum lighting for close work in particular and to wear or use any low vision aids.

*Using a pegboard
in a maths
lesson.* ▶

Eye infections

Childhood eye infections are relatively common. The 'red eye' of conjunctivitis is just one of many. These conditions are easily noticeable by the teacher. Some of these infections are contagious and so care needs to be taken especially with young children. Some infections may arise as secondary conditions linked to childhood illnesses. Treatment is readily available and should be sought. Neglected eye infections can lead to a range of other eye problems such as corneal scarring.

If a child seems to be having unexpected difficulties with visual tasks it is necessary to check with parents but also to observe:

- **does the child have red eyes?**
- **are the eyes watery?**
- **is there evidence of discharge around the eyes?**
- **is the child unusually sensitive to light?**
- **is the child complaining of pain?**

Cataracts

Images are focussed on the retina by the lens. The lens of a healthy eye is clear. When the lens is damaged it responds by becoming 'milky' in appearance. This clouding of the lens (cataract) is not easy to detect without a full eye examination. Like many of the other eye conditions, cataracts may accompany other forms of visual impairment. There are several different types of cataract and the amount of visual loss will vary.

A hand-held magnifier helps access maps in a geography lesson. ▶

Cataracts in children may have been caused by:
- maternal infection (such as German measles)
- hereditary factors (genetic)
- the use of drugs during pregnancy
- trauma (a blow to the eye)

Cataracts are likely to mean:
- the child will be very sensitive to light, *photophobic*
- the child will have reduced visual acuity
- nystagmus may be present
- squints could also be present
- a child may have difficulties with low lighting

Children who are born with cataracts need very early intervention. It is vital that the developing retina obtains light and a clear image. For this reason babies are operated on as soon as possible and affected lenses may be removed. Children therefore could have contact lenses fitted from an early age. If cataracts have developed later then the child may still be receiving treatment whilst at school.

When the cataract has been treated the child will have artificial lenses prescribed. These may be contact lenses or glasses. Close contact will need to be kept with the home so any difficulties over the use of lenses with small children can be avoided. As soon as possible children should be taught how to fit and care for their contact lenses. Teachers may also find it helpful to liaise with the school nurse if one is available.

Albinism

Albinism is a condition which is generally recognised by the distinctive light hair and skin of those affected. It is caused by the congenital lack of pigment in the skin, hair and eyes. Albinism presents a range of difficulties for children:

Looking 'different'
This is a particular problem when children from ethnic minorities, where skin and hair would otherwise be dark, are affected by albinism. Social and behavioural difficulties sometimes arise if children feel excluded or isolated.

Mis-cues
Children suffering from albinism experience the same difficulties as other partially sighted children when trying to use visual cues: facial expressions can be missed or misunderstood. Any emotional problems may be further compounded by this difficulty.

Vision
Normally our eyes are protected from too much light by the coloured iris. In cases of albinism the iris is almost transparent and no longer acts as a light filter. Light enters the eyes in uncomfortable amounts and children will screw up their eyes to avoid this discomfort.

Children with albinism will also have:

- short sight
- nystagmus
- astigmatism

There is no treatment for albinism except to reduce the child's exposure to bright light and the rays of the sun. Skin lacking in pigmentation burns easily. Children may be helped by wearing tinted lenses or contact lenses. They will also need to have their short sight corrected as much as possible. Lenses will not totally resolve the child's visual problems because the retina may not have developed fully. Children may also need the opportunity to talk to a counsellor about any possible feelings of rejection or isolation. In particular children should be helped to deal with racial confusion (looking 'white' in a black family).

Eye size

Children's eyes may sometimes appear to be larger or smaller than their classmates. Mostly this is accounted for as merely individual differences. If it is very obvious then a child may have a developmental anomaly such as 'microphthalmous' (small eyes). There are a variety of reasons why eyes may have restricted growth. Children with microphthalmous will have severe visual impairment.

Eyes which seem very large and are painful may suffer from another developmental anomaly, 'buphthalmous'. Drainage channels at the front of the eye become blocked and pressure builds up in the eye. Pressure in the developing eye means it becomes enlarged. This is a very painful condition. Children will be sensitive to light and complain of headaches. The risk is that the pressure in the eye will lead to a tearing of the retina and very restricted vision. In some extreme cases it may well be necessary to remove the affected eye completely. Ongoing medication will be needed to control problems of intra-ocular pressure. This will usually be given in the form of eyedrops but some drugs can now be administered as slow release from a capsule under the eyelid. This may be an increasing possibility for children in the future and will overcome some of the problems of medication being forgotten.

Developing and deteriorating conditions

Severe visual impairments in children are rare and hopefully will have been diagnosed before the child begins school. This is particularly likely in cases where the eyes look noticeably different. Teachers need to be aware of the implications but any possible treatment is likely to be underway. However, not all eye conditions occur in the early years. Some conditions will deteriorate while the child is attending school and some will develop during the course of a child's education. Most unexpected of all will be accident- or illness-induced vision problems. The more common form of visual difficulty is caused by refractive errors (see below).

The routine screening of children's eyes is tremendously important. Not only are healthy eyes necessary for children to access everyday learning material, but eyes give an indication as to the general wellbeing of the child. Eye conditions which are difficult to detect other than by routine screening tend to be the refractive anomalies which cause long and short sight.

Children suffering from conditions such as diabetes will need very regular monitoring and special attention should be given to children whose vision seems to fluctuate or who complain of fuzzy images. The class teacher plays a very important role in this monitoring as children already known to have some special needs may possibly have undiagnosed additional problems. Even minor visual problems can compound other learning difficulties.

Refractive anomalies

In the pre-school and early years children are very much involved in gross play and activities involving brightly coloured toys and objects. Play tends to be centred around the home and familiar surroundings. Unless a child has a very severe visual impairment, they will find visual strategies to suit the needs of the pre-school environment. This means that it is harder to assess the functional vision of very young children.

When the child gets older and starts school they are likely to be moving to a less familiar environment. Visual tasks will be much more specifically guided by the teacher. Learning to read and write is very specific indeed. Working from printed material and from information displayed at some distance all adds to the complexity of visual tasks. Children who seemed to have no visual difficulties will begin to exhibit problems. For this reason vision screening should normally take place as a child begins formal schooling. There is a particular role for teachers in the early primary phase of school to be aware of the effect poor vision will have on the acquisition of reading and writing skills.

An angled worksurface and talking calculator in use for a maths lesson. ▶

Short sight

Short sight 'myopia' is caused by the abnormal length of the eyeball. The visual image falls short of the retina. A child with short sight will have a particular difficulty with tasks presented at a distance. The distance at which this difficulty occurs will depend on the severity of the short sight as well as the type of material and lighting involved. Children will not be aware of their short sight until it has been corrected by the use of lenses. So they will not usually complain of visual difficulties but you may find that they will try to move closer to any distant source of information.

A child with short sight is likely to:

- have problems with hand-eye co-ordination and may withdraw from games involving the use of balls or distant targets.
- be poor at physical activities because of restricted visual information for copying body position.
- spend more time on desktop activities (traditionally children with short sight have been considered as overly studious by their peers).

Perkins brailler (foreground) and beyond it, a laptop with speech output. ▶

30

In most instances short sight becomes more significant as the eyeball develops. There are a few cases where the short sight beomes so severe that there is a danger that the retina will be torn or detached. This sort of short sight is called 'high myopia'. Because of the possibility of deterioration, children with short sight should be regularly screened.

Treatment for short sight is still largely dependent on the prescription of lenses which will compensate for the length of the eyeball. Contact lenses are popular but children do find difficulties with keeping them clean and often loose them. Nevertheless contact lenses do offer a more comfortable option for children involved in sport than traditional glasses. There has been increasing interest recently in the use of surgery to correct short sight but at present this is unlikely to be recommended for children. Traditional prejudice against glasses has been reduced by their inclusion as fashion accessories but there does remain some reluctance to wearing them. Young children especially will be reluctant. For them the benefits do not necessarily outweigh the inconvenience.

Once children have become used to their corrected vision they will experience visual blurring when lenses are removed. This does not mean that their eyes are being weakened by the use of lenses but rather that their visual perception has to adapt to the improved clarity of image when lenses are worn and vice versa.

Long sight

Long sight, 'hypermetropia', is caused by the shortness of the eyeball. The lens may also be weak. Babies tend to be longsighted, although this tendency would normally disappear as the child reaches 24 months in age. In long sight the child will hold objects close to their eyes but will have little difficulty with objects in the distance. This means that the eyes will converge (turn inwards). Young children have the ability to bring their eyes very closely inwards in order to focus on a near object. As children get older the eyes loose this power to converge closely. Therefore a child who has been able to cope with long sight in the early years will have increasing problems in later schooling.

> **Using the eyes to converge on objects is tiring. Children with long sight like those with short sight are unlikely to be aware of their visual problem but may complain of:**
>
> - **tiredness after visual tasks**
> - **headaches**

Teachers may notice that the child seems easily distracted and lacks concentration. Lenses will correct this condition. Long sight tends to be a more stable condition than short sight. Long sight is often associated with squints and astigmatism.

Astigmatism

Normally the cornea is smooth and rounded. Astigmatism occurs when for any reason the cornea becomes uneven. There are several forms of astigmatism starting with the relatively common simple astigmatism. This is where there is only one part of the cornea affected and the resulting blurring of vision can be easily corrected. The more complex forms will require a mixture of lenses and vision training. For children an astigmatism can make reading difficult, particularly if the astigmatism is in association with other conditions such as long or short sight.

> **The teacher will need to monitor the effectiveness of the lenses prescribed for the child by the observation of:**
>
> - the child's preferred reading position
> - whether the child prefers to work without spectacles
> - the child's handwriting
> - whether the child can read back their own handwriting

In addition to the refractive errors, which are relatively common forms of minor visual problems there are the more general difficulties related to colour and light.

Colour confusion

Commonly though misleadingly known as 'colour blindness' colour confusion affects around 8 per cent of males. Males suffering from colour confusion outnumber females by about 20 to 1. The most common form of confusion is between red, yellow and green. Children suffering from colour confusion are likely to have particular difficulties with maps and any diagrammatic representations (such as circuitry) where colour coding is used. Road safety is important and children may need to learn specifically about colour configurations used in traffic lights.

Difficulties with light and shade

Many visual problems will also have attendant difficulties relating to light. Some children will be very sensitive to bright light. Such sensitivity is known as 'photophobia'. These children will perform better in rooms without too much direct light or glare. Some will even prefer low lighting conditions.

Night blindness is also a feature of some visual impairments. Children will have increasing problems as light decreases and will have virtually no functional vision in low lighting. Night blindness is not easy to detect as children may perform adequately throughout the school day. Teachers are unlikely to be aware of any difficulties a child has after dark. Young children would not be expected to be out alone in the evening and so their real difficulties do not emerge until adolescence when school and family may notice unusual behaviours in the child.

Because the child will be unaware that they have a visual problem they do not know why they feel worried about activities in the evening. Teachers might be alerted if a child has difficulties in the winter term when light fades before the end of the school day. Children can seem particularly stressed at this time of year and may have a number of minor accidents. It is important that night blindness is detected not only for the safety of the child but because the condition can be an indicator of more substantial visual impairments.

Current concerns

As children with complex needs are more commonly placed in mainstream provision so the range of visual impairments which class and support teachers encounter will also become more complex.

Cortical visual impairment

One of the aspects of visual functioning which is currently being researched is the late development of vision experienced by some children. These children have apparently healthy and normally functioning eyes and yet they may perform as though totally blind. Children with this type of need are described as cortically visually impaired. Visual impairment is caused by damage to the visual cortex in the brain.

Research into cortical visual impairment carried out in America and Canada suggests that about 70 per cent of functionally blind children with other disabilities suffer from cortical impairment. With careful and structured training it would seem that these children can develop the use of their vision. Although some children's vision will develop completely, others will remain severely visually impaired but will gain the use of some residual vision. The experience of work being carried out with these children may well help us to understand more about the development of visual perception in the brain. Learning about the types of visual stimulation programmes which seem to help cortically visually impaired children may help us more generally to make vision training available.

Low birth weight

More children are surviving with very low birth weights. A condition which is associated with babies of birth weights less than 1500g or new born babies exposed to oxygen for prolonged periods is retinopathy of prematurity (ROP). Because babies are surviving with lower and lower birthweights it is now more common for ROP to be part of a range of other profound physical and neurological impairments. Intervention is available for some types of ROP. Treatment would be undertaken long before school age. Schools would need to be advised on the level of functional vision displayed by the child on school entry as well as the likely prognosis for visual development.

CHAPTER 3

ASSESSMENT OF VISION

The 1993 Education Act and its Code of Practice rightly places great importance on the thorough and ongoing assessment of children with special educational needs. Severe visual impairment as with other types of disability needs to be assessed both clinically and educationally.

There are several components of assessment of vision which are used to:
- determine the clinical picture
- gain a functional perspective
- identify appropriate provision.

These various aspects of assessment are not necessarily discrete and in many cases will overlap. This sometimes makes establishing the roles of the various professionals involved quite difficult. A child may be identified as having a potential visual problem in the first few days or weeks after birth, or many months or years may elapse. For the purposes of understanding reports received by the school, one can separate the types of visual assessment into two elements; clinical and functional.

Information obtained from medical sources may sometimes include functional components but will tend to focus on the clinical presentation of the child's eye condition. For this reason a child will often be assessed clinically as having very little vision whilst parents and school may feel that these assessments underestimate the child's actual functional vision.

Because of the unique and individual way children respond to a visual impairment it is misleading to assume that any two children who present with a similar eye condition will exhibit the same levels of functional vision. Assessment and early intervention are therefore important both from the clinical and functional points of view.

From a medical perspective the early detection of a severe visual impairment is important because:

- **treatment may be available which could reduce or eliminate the effects of some conditions.**
- **genetic counselling may be required so parents understand the implications for other siblings.**
- **parents may need information and advice on developmental implications.**
- **problems with vision may be an indication of serious illness.**

From an educational perspective early detection is also important because:

- parents may need help and advice on support services available.
- parents may need advice to help the child maximize their use of any residual vision.
- specialist help for early mobility training, physiotherapy, or speech therapy may be needed.
- adequate support for nursery and pre-school provision will need to be identified.
- low vision aids and equipment may need to provided.
- formal assessment procedures under the 1993 Act and the Children Act may need to be instigated.

Clinical assessment

There are likely to be a number of professionals involved in clinical assessments and children may be referred for assessment from a variety of sources depending on their age. The following professionals are most likely to be involved:

Pediatrician
Concerned with the general development of the child. Some eye hospitals have pediatricians who specialise in the needs of children with visual impairments. The paediatrician will work with the ophthalmologist.

Ophthalmologist
Will be a qualified surgeon specialising in conditions affecting vision. Because eye conditions are often part of more general medical conditions the ophthalmologist will sometimes have a wider involvement and will assess:

- refraction
- eye movements
- developmental anomalies
- general eye health
- any systemic implications

The ophthalmologist can also 'register' someone as blind. Registration is the mechanism by which a visually impaired person can claim entitlement to some specific benefits. The Consultant Ophthalmologist completes a registration form which is sent to Social Services. The registration level of blindness is a visual acuity of 3/60 or worse (see page 38 for an explanation of these figures). A child with a severe field loss (see page 40) would also be considered. Registration is not compulsory. Very few children are actually registered because benefits seem more related to adult needs. Also, some families and clinicians feel childhood might be too early to be definite about a child's ultimate level of visual functioning.

Orthoptist

Works with children who have abnormal eye movements such as squints. Because of the importance of binocular vision the work of the orthoptist is a crucial part of both clinical and functional assessment. The orthoptist will recommend eye exercises to help children develop effective eye movements. Orthoptists may also be involved in primary screening, and are often part of a multi-disciplinary assessment team.

General practitioner

Although the GP would not normally be involved in sight testing they are an important link between services. Many visual problems have an underlying medical disorder so liaison between services is especially important.

The clinical report

The following shows the sort of information which might be sent by an ophthalmologist as a contribution to advice for a full assessment:

> **The patient has been seen at this hospital since he was eight months old when he presented with a left convergent squint and high levels of hypermetropia, more marked on the right side. He had left squint surgery in May 1986 and has had spectacles and occlusion therapy over the intervening years. In July 1993, he had further surgical treatment to the left eye for consecutive exotropia.**
>
> **At his latest post operative visit on 28th July 1993 he had right vision 6/9, left vision 6/36 with good ocular alignment the majority of the time.**
>
> **The patient has adequate vision on the right side, he has left amblyopia which will not respond to treatment at his age. He has vision which is adequate for his schooling.**

This type of report is far from easy to understand. An explanation of terms is given on page 47. One of the main roles of the peripatetic teacher for visually impaired children is to help parents and school understand the medical terminology. More importantly, they would also use this information as background to their own assessment of the child's functional vision.

Functional assessment

Most of us will have had some experience of having our eyes tested. Those of us who wear spectacles have ongoing contact with sight tests through the work of ophthalmic opticians. The number of spectacle and lens wearers can be judged by the frequency of optician's shops in any high street. In an aging and increasingly deskbound population optical services are a growth industry. There are also services provided by hospital departments where low vision clinics will be used by children who have been referred by an ophthalmologist. The roles of those involved in these services sometimes overlap.

Optometrist
An Optometrist is concerned with assessing refractive errors. They can prescribe and provide lenses or vision training.

Ophthalmic optician
As well as dispensing lenses an ophthalmic optician is trained to assess functional vision. Like the optometrist the ophthalmic optician is not qualified to treat medical conditions.

Dispensing optician
The dispensing optician will make up the prescription issued by the ophthalmic optician. They will also ensure that the fit of lenses is correct. Sometimes dispensing opticians will work in liaison with an ophthalmologist in a medical eye centre.

Peripatetic teacher
Will perform functional vision assessments in school or for pre-school children in the home but does not prescribe or fit lenses.

What happens in a vision assessment?

Whether the assessment is conducted in a hospital or in an ophthalmic optician's examination room, there are basic procedures which will be carried out. There will be regard to the optimum conditions for visual functioning and standard testing procedures.

Distance vision
The chart most commonly associated with sight testing is the 'Snellen' chart. This chart has a series of letters starting with the largest at the top and subsequent rows of letters arranged in decreasing order of size.

Each line of letters on the Snellen chart has a corresponding number which relates to the distance such a letter could be read by a normally functioning eye. For

The Snellen chart is the most common method of testing distance vision. Symbols and pictures can be used with young children. ▶

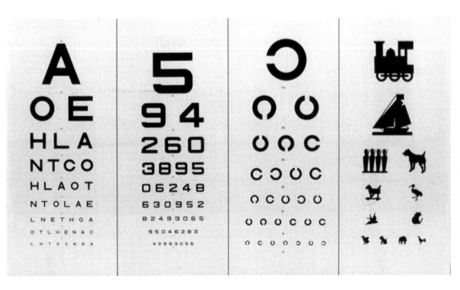

example, the top line corresponds to a distance of 60 metres, the next line 36, on until 6, 5, and 4 metres are reached. The usual testing distance is 6 metres. The last complete line that the person can read indicates their level of visual acuity and this is then recorded. If an individual had a difficulty with even the top line (which is large enough to be seen at 60 metres) they would move closer until they could read it and that distance would be recorded. The patient starts from the top of the chart with the largest letter and works downwards.

As a sort of shorthand the test is only ever written as a series of numbers. The first number indicates the distance at which the person was able to read that particular line on the chart. The second number is the distance at which that line would be read by someone with normal visual acuity. Because testing takes place at 6 metres the Snellen line which can be read at the standard distance of 6 metres is used as a base line. Standard visual acuity is therefore recorded as 6/6.

6/36 = The distance at which this person was able to read the Snellen line was 6 metres and this was the last line on the chart they could accurately read. This line, however, would be read by a person with normal vision at 36 metres. A child with this measurement of visual acuity would need to have further investigation if they were not already being seen by an ophthalmologist.

6/18 = The distance at which this person was able to read the Snellen line was 6 metres and this was the last line they could accurately read. This line, however, would be read by a person with normal vision at 18 metres. A child with this level of acuity would also need to be checked by an ophthalmologist.

3/60 = The distance at which the person tested was able to read this Snellen line was 3 metres and this was the last line on the chart they could accurately read. This line, however, would be read by a person with normal vision at 60 metres. A child with this measurement of vision could be registered as blind.

If the child has had glasses or contact lenses prescribed they will be assessed using this correction to their vision. Reports will sometimes indicate whether vision was 'corrected' when the test was conducted and the Snellen figure may appear "R6/60 corrected." This means that the child's vision in the right eye was 6/60 and that they were wearing lenses (either contact or glasses). The Snellen figure does not take account of any peripheral (side) loss of vision so a child with a condition where their central vision remained very acute could seem to have fairly normal vision. Therefore Snellen figures will appear with the results of other tests.

Near vision

Assessment of near vision is carried out by means of the N print test. The person being tested will look at a series of cards each with a number relating to the standard print type size used. This test is carried out at around 25cm but can be varied according to the preferred viewing distance of the person being tested. As with the Snellen chart the N print test starts with the larger print sizes and then the print size is reduced. The smallest print size which can be comfortably read is then recorded. A person with normal vision using good clear print would be able to read N5 at 25cms.

The N print test includes type in many different sizes. ▶

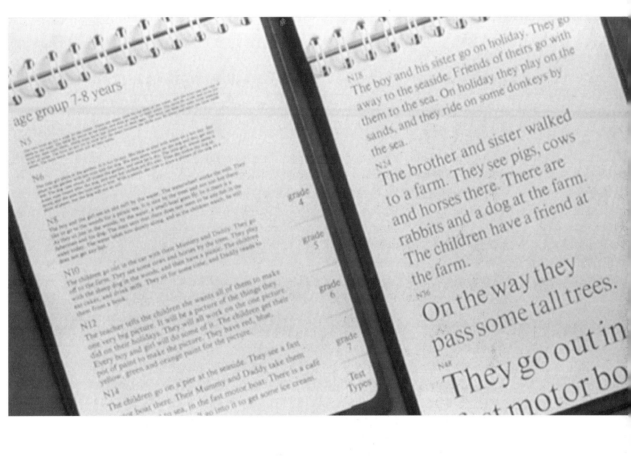

Visual fields

As well as testing near and distance vision it is important to assess the child's visual field. A visual field is the amount of all round vision a child has. This includes side as well as central vision. This means that any gaps in vision will be indicated. Conditions such as hemionopia where half the visual field may be lost are particularly important for reading where a child's ability to scan will be seriously affected. Other conditions may leave the child with good central vision but very little side (peripheral) vision. This may mean the child has problems in their movement and can appear clumsy or trip and fall easily.

Colour and depth perception

It is also important to gain an accurate idea of any other problems a child might have. Difficulties over colour discrimination are not uncommon and so the child will have their colour vision assessed as well as their depth perception.

Comparison tests

There may be differences or discrepancies in the appearance or functioning of individual eyes. This will be particularly marked if the child has a squint for example. Assessment will indicate whether treatment would be beneficial and whether the child should be given vision training.

Eye movements

Eye movements may be affected by a variety of medical conditions or congenital abnormalities. There has been increasing interest in the relationship between abnormal eye movements and reading difficulties. This is not easy to detect and there are continuing disagreements between ophthalmologists as to the overall importance of eye movements in relation to specific learning difficulties. It remains an important area of concern, for without co-ordinated eye movements the child will not develop effective binocular vision.

Medical and family history

The child's family history is important when looking at the possibility of inherited anomalies or genetic implications, as is the child's current state of health. If the child is being treated for any illness there may be visual problems associated as side effects from the medication itself as well as from the medical condition.

Why testing may be difficult

Assessment of vision is carried out at all ages and stages of life. Very young children and those with additional learning disabilities are difficult to assess and so reports received by the school are likely to be harder to interpret. A child's functioning can be affected by so many external factors. Vision is no exception. There are many adaptations to tests which take account of the child's age, level of literacy and so on. What is particularly hard to disentangle from the assessment of young children is the inter-relationship between cognition, perception and sight.

This is where the role of the parent, peripatetic vision specialist and classroom teacher is so crucial. They observe the child regularly and will see any changes in her behaviour. They will also be familiar with any strategies the child adopts to cope with her visual impairment. Never be afraid therefore to challenge a report on a child's vision, but do back up 'hunches' with consistent observation of the child in a variety of situations.

Symbol cubes or cards standardised to Snellen sizes can be used to test very young children or those with learning disabilities ▶

Where can Special Educational Needs Co-ordinators go for advice?

Ideally the needs of a severely visually impaired child would be identified early. There will be instances, however, when a child's eye condition has developed during the school years or a child may have suffered illness or accident which has affected their vision. In these instances the school may be the first place that the child's real difficulties are highlighted. Parents will need to be alerted and the child should be taken to their General Practitioner to make sure there are no medical problems. The child will then be referred to an ophthalmologist.

Voluntary organisations such as the Royal National Institute for the Blind (RNIB) or local voluntary groups will often be a useful source of information for schools and parents. Advocacy support for parents can be obtained through the voluntary sector.

From the school's perspective the child has a special educational need which has to be addressed. Support services are currently being restructured and key contact points will differ. Even where schools no longer use their local authority services for learning support there will be a need to seek specialist advice for children with visual impairments.

The peripatetic teacher

Peripatetic teachers for visually impaired children are fully qualified teachers who have undertaken an extra period of training to work with visually impaired children and have obtained a mandatory specialist qualification. Although they are usually employed by local education authorities they operate as a link between community health services, social services and education.

The peripatetic teacher will:
- **perform functional but not clinical assessments paying special attention to helping parents and schools understand the developmental implications of a severe visual impairment.**
- **provide specific information on local and national provision for visually impaired children.**
- **give guidance on the use of low vision aids and other specialised equipment.**
- **offer ongoing support during a child's education.**
- **advise on the appropriate form of written communication for the child (braille or print size).**
- **work with classroom and support staff to ensure that examination and National Curriculum requirements are appropriately adapted to meet the needs of the child.**
- **advise on any environmental adaptations.**
- **assist the child to maximise their use of any residual vision.**
- **work with other specialists such as mobility officers.**
- **contribute to the formal assessment of a child who is visually impaired.**

Special Educational Needs Co-ordinators will also need to seek the advice of the peripatetic teacher to ensure appropriate levels of any ongoing support required by the child.

Assessment: the classroom perspective

The peripatetic teacher for visually impaired children will be particularly concerned to assess how the child is using their vision in the classroom and will want to discuss any particular difficulties or needs staff in the school have identified. The child should be an active partner in these discussions. This form of assessment of functional vision is to determine the educational implications of the child's visual impairment and to identify any resource implications as well as any teaching approaches (the way material is presented for example) or environmental considerations (lighting or desk position etc.).

The peripatetic teacher would normally only assess those children with a severe visual loss. This means that children whose sight is corrected by the use of lenses to a level where no other intervention is required would not usually be assessed. This type of functional assessment does not have the formality of a clinical assessment nor does it have the ideal testing conditions provided by an ophthalmologist. This is important because the peripatetic teacher is interested in the daily school experience of the child and how they cope when visual conditions are likely to be far from ideal!

The assessment will pay particular regard to general factors including:

- the age of the child.
- the clinical assessment provided by the ophthalmologist.
- reports on a child's overall progress at school.
- parental concerns and observations.
- discussion with the child.
- the observations of the class teacher.
- the general health of the child and school attendance.
- any medication being taken by the child.
- any lenses the child is currently using to improve visual acuity.
- the classroom and school environment.
- any additional disabilities or needs displayed by the child.
- the time the child takes to complete work.
- the way a child approaches a visual task.
- the child's preferred angle and viewing distance.
- the general movement and posture of the child.
- hand-eye co-ordination.

Activities and assessment materials will be determined by the age and developmental level of the child as well as the range of classroom activities most usually performed by the child. Assessment materials will be chosen to be interesting and rewarding so the child is motivated and engaged by them. The sequence of assessment is also important and how it relates to the school day. Tasks requiring the child to use fine visual discrimination may be more successful if the child has previously been physically active and is generally feeling alert. The child's general range of experience will be taken into account when presenting material which the child may otherwise fail to recognise. If photographs of people are used they should include images of individuals from the child's own ethnic group.

Samples of the child's work will be helpful especially from a mix of both creative and prescribed sources. Young children are usually keen to discuss their drawing and painting. Older children may be prepared to discuss their written work.

Aspects considered in a vision assessment

The child's responses:
- how the child reacts to light
- how the child's eyes move
- the child's shifting gaze
- how efficiently the child tracks and scans
- blinking reflex
- does the child screw up her eyes when looking?

Two-dimensional schoolwork
Drawing, painting:
- whether the child recognises her own work
- if the child tires easily when engaged in colouring or drawing
- whether the child can copy from life
- if the child misses out parts of the drawing
- if the child superimposes line on line
- how the child holds a pen or pencil
- what colours the child prefers and how easily the child recognises these colours
- whether the child can use colouring books
- how close does the child get to her work?

Writing:
- how well the child can write
- whether letters are missed, reversed or confused beyond a usual expectation in a child of that age
- the size of the child's writing
- if the child can copy from a near source
- whether the child can copy from a blackboard, whiteboard or wallchart

Reading:
- whether the child can read
- if the child scans easily or with difficulty
- the size of print the child reads easily
- if the child uses her finger to keep her place in the text
- whether the child can read back her own writing
- if the child recognises photographs of objects and people

Three-dimensional schoolwork
- whether the child recognises similar and individual differences between objects
- if the child identifies the size of objects without touch
- if the child identifies one object in a group of several without touch
- whether the child can track a moving object
- the child's ability to judge distances between objects

Movement:
- bearing in mind the child's age what is the child's level of body awareness?
- is the child reluctant to move?
- how confidently does the child move?
- does the child's physical confidence vary?
- does the child stumble or trip more than their peers?
- does the child have difficulties with games involving moving objects, such as balls?

Once the peripatetic teacher has completed the functional assessment she will use this as a basis for determining the approaches most suitable for reducing the child's difficulties. This may mean a recommendation for further medical intervention and assessment, or the sort of equipment and teaching approaches which will reduce the child's difficulties. If the child is the subject of a formal Statement of Special Needs the peripatetic teacher will contribute to the Statement. Responsibility for providing equipment and other resources as well as its management will also need to be identified.

Vision training and stimulation

We have all experienced conditions in which our vision has been reduced; poor lighting, excessive glare from the sun or snow. Similarly there are other conditions which make our visual tasks easier; clear print in books or magazines, a bright colour against a dark background. Designers of modern office environments are now much more aware of the need to provide daylight adjusted lighting and good on-task lighting for individual workstations. If those of us with good vision can be helped by environmental adjustments it must be logical to assume that children with poor vision can be similarly helped but for them the effects may be more dramatic.

Because vision can be subject to delay in some children early intervention and vision training is important. Work with cortically blind children (where the eye itself is unimpaired but the visual cortex is affected) has shown that many of these children can develop useful vision. Traditionally children with squints have undergone training to help with eye alignment.

Stimulation and training of a child's vision does need to:

- take account of the child's medical condition
- have a functional basis
- be informed by knowledge of normal visual development
- allow sufficient time for the child's visual response
- be meaningful for the child
- use the child's normal environment
- make use of appropriate visual aids where these have been prescribed
- be a partnership between school and home

Visual stimulation is implicit in most nursery and infant phase teaching but severely visually impaired children will need longer to respond or to be taught to move their eyes or head to achieve the best possible viewing angle. They will also need help with sensory integration so that looking, touching and listening are combined to offer maximum information. A good visual environment will help all children.

A laptop computer with speech output ▶

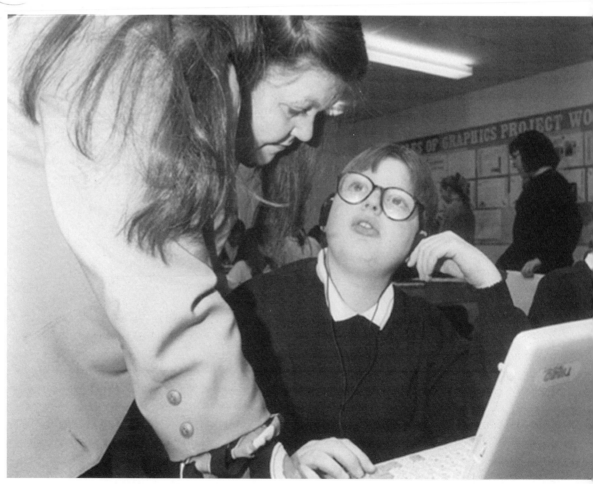

Some terms likely to be found in reports on vision

Accommodation: Ability of the eye to focus at different distances.

Acuity: Clarity or sharpness of vision.

Adaptation: The ability of the eye to adjust to varying amounts of light.

Binocular vision: Ability to use both eyes simultaneously to fuse the image from each eye into one.

Bilateral: Two sided (affects both eyes.)

Blindness: Registration for blindness is carried out by the ophthalmologist using form BD8. The legal definition of blindness comes from the 1948 National Assistance Act which classifies functional blindness in three ways:

1. Visual acuity below 3/60

2. 3/60 but below 6/60 with a very contracted field of vision

3. 6/60 or above but with a very contracted field of vision (see page 38 for an explanation of these figures). Very few children are registered as blind though this position may change under the Children Act. Registration carries some benefits but at present these tend to favour adult needs.

Congenital: Present at birth.

Convergence: Process of directing the visual axes of the two eyes to a near point with the result that the pupils move closer together.

Count fingers (CF): The child who cannot see the Snellen Chart is assessed by the ophthalmologist holding their fingers in front of the child. The distance the child is able to count the fingers is then recorded.

Diplopia: The seeing of one object as two.

Distance vision: The ability to see objects clearly from a distance.

Educationally blind: The primary source of information is through auditory and tactile channels.

Enucleation: Complete surgical removal of the eyeball.

Eye dominance: Tendency of one eye to assume the lead in seeing and the other eye to assist the dominant one.

Familial: Traceable in the family history.

Field of vision: The entire area that can be seen.

Fixation: The ability to direct gaze on an object and hold the object in view.

Hand movements (HM): The measurement of visual response for children who cannot see the Snellen chart or see enough to count fingers.

Hypermetropia: Long sight.

Light adaptation: The ability of the eye to change and adjust to varying amounts of light.

Light perception (LP): Ability to perceive light from dark.

Low vision: Partial sight.

Monocular: Referring to one eye.

Myopia: Short sight.

Oculus dexter (OD): Right eye.

Oculus sinister (OS): Left eye.

Oculus unitas (OU): Both eyes.

Partially sighted: No legal definition but usually taken to mean an acuity of 6/60 or less.

Peripheral vision: Perception of objects, motion or colour by any part of the retina except the central macula area.

Photophobia: Extreme sensitivity to light.

Saccadic fixation: Jumping movement of the eye between fixations.

Scotoma: Blind or partially sighted spot in the visual field.

Sine correction (SC): Without correction. (eg. not wearing glasses).

Tunnel vision: Only central vision remaining.

CHAPTER 4

SUPPORTING THE CHILD IN SCHOOL

Visually impaired children attending their local mainstream school will require a range of support. Some children will need only careful monitoring whilst others will need individual support, specialised equipment and training. Generally it is true to say that congenitally blind children will need substantial human and technological resources if they are to have full access to the curriculum. Children with low vision may also need specialised equipment in addition to modified learning materials and individual support.

Learning and communication

Providing access to the curriculum for a child with a severe visual impairment presents obvious challenges to the mainstream school. The most substantial challenge is related to the provision of a method of communication appropriate to the child's needs. This is not easy because so much teaching is dependent on visual means. Making a successful choice between educating a child using sighted or alternative approaches will depend on the amount and use the child can make of their residual vision. Decisions relating to whether the preferred medium will be print or tactile have to take into consideration a range of issues including familial acceptance of the child's functioning, the importance of children using their remaining vision (however limited) rather than more efficient alternative approaches.

To some children and families braille is the final recognition that the child is blind and children who have lost their sight more recently may find the suggestion that they learn braille too traumatic. However, there are also children who welcome braille as a relief from their struggle to use an inappropriate sighted medium. Teachers need to be sensitive when helping the child choose an appropriate medium either for long or short term use.

Reading a braille version of the class novel with support from a cassette tape. ▶

Braille

For an educationally blind child the medium required for reading will be a tactile or auditory one. For writing the option is likely to be braille. Braille, like the white cane, is almost a symbol of blindness. Most people know that blind people use raised dots for reading and are fascinated by the process. Braille is indeed a system of writing and reading which is based on six raised dots. As a code it is a mixture of letter for letter transcription (Grade 1) and a series of abbreviations much like shorthand (Grade 2).

The traditional means of braille production is the Perkins Brailler. Some people refer to the Perkins as a braille typewriter but this is misleading. The Perkins does not have a keyboard like a conventional typewriter or word processor but six keys which produce the necessary dots or braille 'cells'. Each letter or abbreviation is made from a combination of these cells. Like print, braille is read from left to right. Studies have shown that the most efficient braille reading is accomplished by using the index fingers on both hands. The National Curriculum does not include statutory requirements for braille but non-statutory guidelines are available from the RNIB.

Using a Perkins Brailler. ▶

Braille is a complex code which is difficult to learn. When planning the child's Individual Education Programme (IEP) sufficient time will need to be allocated. In addition, there will be the need for support from experienced staff who understand the teaching of braille. Learning to read and write braille efficiently is dependent on the combination of tactual and cognitive skills.

Children will need the opportunity to develop:

- gross motor skills
- fine motor skills
- tactile discrimination
- hand and finger strength
- braille reading readiness

Because of the lack of incidental learning experienced by educationally blind children it is important to be very structured when teaching braille. Braille reading schemes therefore seem very traditional. Children need to develop significant motivation to learn braille and acquire different strategies to those which sighted children would use when learning to read print. Pictures are integral to early reading books but these are not available to blind children. Alternatives have to be found which can stimulate the child's imagination and interest. Raised pictures or drawings are not easily recognised by touch and do not automatically replace illustrations. Congenitally blind children do not find the use of models a replacement for pictures because a tactile experience of any real object cannot be easily represented in model form.

The need to respond to this challenge has produced some very exciting developments. These include:

- **the use of a variety of objects and textures in place of illustrations**
- **audio cassettes using music or sound cues**
- **shared reading opportunities for braille and print readers such as the 'ClearVision' books which combine braille and print (for more information on ClearVision books, contact the address on page 71).**

The beauty of such schemes is their simplicity and accessibility. Teachers involved in helping children learn braille should undertake a specialist training in braille themselves. Once children have become proficient braille readers they can join a braille lending library through the RNIB and have books sent to them at home or at school.

Moon

Until relatively recently Moon was not considered as an option for children. Moon is based on the print alphabet and is made up of straight and curved raised lines. It

Examples of Moon. ▶

The Moon Alphabet

Moon characters can be produced in a range of font

24 point

36 point

48 point

60 point

Numerals

(Number sign)

1 2 3 4 5 6 7 8 9 0

Can you read this sentence in Moon?

was developed for adults who had lost their sight in later life and who had learned to read using the print alphabet. Like braille there is an abbreviated form.

Some children do find braille very difficult to learn and Moon has been used as an alternative to braille for children with additional disabilities. The advantage of Moon over braille for children with tactual problems is that it can be enlarged and give an enhanced tactual experience without losing its shape and structure. Braille has to be read by using the pad of the finger. Spacing between braille cells has been found to be optimum and although jumbo braille does exist it becomes a totally different reading experience for the child.

One disadvantage of Moon is that there is no means for children easily writing it, although a computer programme has recently been developed which may offer increased possibilities. The 'Moonwriter' which was invented to provide access to Moon production is extremely complex and time consuming for children to use. The other major disadvantage of Moon for children is the scarcity of appropriate reading materials. For more information about Moon, contact the address given on page 71.

Print

Most visually impaired children in mainstream schools have some useful vision. For the child with low vision the communication medium used is likely to be print.

> **When writing, children with low vision may experience:**
>
> - a difficulty with pen or pencil control
> - a tendency to miss out words or part of words
> - a confusion over letter orientation and so may reverse letters for a longer period than a fully sighted child.
> - difficulty reading back their own work

The sort of print the child will need depends on a number of factors.

Eye condition
Some children will require the print size enlarged and the density of the print line increased whilst others will function better with reduced print size. There are eye conditions which will produce fluctuating levels of vision and so the child's requirements can change.

Cognitive and Conceptual functioning
Any additional learning disability will have a very marked effect on a visually impaired child's ability to develop strategies to cope with reading print or braille. Children with additional needs may therefore require a range of resources to reinforce their 'looking' and 'thinking' skills. It may help to establish a programme based on early visual development. This will encourage the child to establish good tracking, scanning and visual closure (the ability to look at a half-formed or partial image and complete it).

Age

Children who are in the early stages of learning to read will already have access to most of their material in large print. They will also not be expected to concentrate for long periods. As children get older the size of print is normally reduced and they are expected to concentrate for increasing periods of time. For children who find visual tasks tiring, the problem can be compounded. The range of material easily and independently accessible to the child also significantly decreases. Reading for leisure is thus restricted, potentially isolating the child from peer reading interests such as material presented in magazines and comics.

Task

The typeface and size of print accessible to the child will be influenced by the overall layout of a piece of text as well as the actual content. If, for instance, a child is required to use a book to gather reference material then the presentation of tables and graphs as well as their position in the text will influence the child's ability to manage the print size. The use of illustrations and drawings in the text may also confuse the child particularly if they have difficulty scanning. A child with scanning problems is more likely to lose their place in the text.

Tasks that require the child to have access to distance material will also need to be considered in relation to print size as would sharing of any written material. Generally it is not advisable for a visually impaired child to share reading materials, but the teacher may wish to encourage group activities and so it is sometimes essential that the child engages in shared reading tasks. Presentation should follow general principles of using clear, uncluttered print and layout. Being conscious of the quality of learning materials offered will help all the children in the school.

A 'ClearVision' book combines a clear braille overlay with the printed text and pictures. ▶

The environment

Sadly many school environments are far from ideal places for teaching and learning. Schools built during the last century are often dark and difficult to heat and light. Power sockets are few and far between. Newer schools with large amounts of glass may expose the child to glare.

On-task lighting as well as good ambient lighting can change a visually impossible task into an achievable one. As can the provision of blinds (which are in working order) by reducing the intensity of light for children suffering from photophobia. A child who may be reading with considerable discomfort can find herself not only more comfortable but with an improved reading speed if lighting conditions are appropriate for the task.

Contrast sensitivity

It will also help if the child's contrast sensitivity is assessed. Some children will function better with black print on a coloured background or with a colour filter over the text whilst others may find white print against a dark background especially helpful. The kind of paper used will have a bearing on the child's contrast sensitivity. Shiny paper is more likely to give rise to problems with glare. The position of reading material is also important. Some children are more comfortable using reading stands although many children are reluctant to use apparatus which singles them out as different from the rest of the class.

Possible solutions

Low vision aids

Low vision aids can be divided into low- and high-tech optical solutions. At the simplest level the use of a pen which gives a thick enough line or is dark enough may help. It can also be useful to outline black print with colour if the child has cortical

A low-tech aid, available from the RNIB. ▶

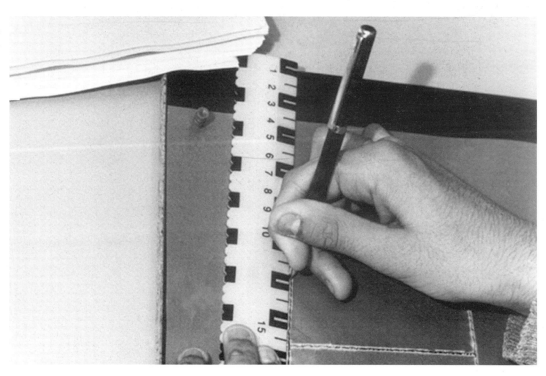

problems, for instance. Spectacles are another example of a low-tech approach especially if kept clean! In addition to spectacles the use of lenses in a range of magnifiers and microscopes can also help. For near tasks such as print reading there are hand-held, stand and spectacle attached types of aid. For those requiring help with distance viewing of charts and black or whiteboards similar devices are available.

There are advantages and disadvantages in the use of low vision aids. At best they provide access to material and tasks which would not be possible without them. But children do need to be taught to use them correctly. It is worth noting that the amount of magnification used will affect the child's field of vision. High levels of magnification thus reduce the child's speed of scanning and tracking, making reading comparatively slow and laborious. The working distance from materials is also reduced and there is an increased need to focus accurately on specific areas.

Young children are likely to find low vision aids hard to manage so will need extra help until they have developed the necessary physical skills.

High tech versions of optical aids are closed circuit televisions with hand held or integral cameras as well as computer generated large or small print on screen.

Presentation and production of learning materials

How materials are modified and presented to children will depend on:

- **the purpose of the materials**
- **what the teaching point of the material is**
- **an assessment of the most accessible and acceptable form of presentation**
- **the availability of resources and staff knowledge of equipment use**
- **the time available for the child to use the material**
- **the time taken to produce the material and how much it will be used**
- **how the material is to be used**
- **the skills needed by the child to access the material**
- **the level of support the child needs to use the material**

Preparing teaching materials with thermoform. ▶

The use of diagrams

Diagrams pose problems for both blind and partially sighted children. Partially sighted children using high levels of magnification will find scanning maps and diagrams difficult. Time will need to be spent presenting only the essential aspects of any diagram. Labelling needs to be carefully thought through as excessive amounts of information can confuse the child and take valuable time away from the main task. The blind child will need access to tactile diagrams (these can also help some partially sighted children). There are several methods of production including the use of commercial kits which offer a mix of textured materials, collage provided from the teacher's scrap box as well as specialist papers and implements, but the two most common forms of duplication are:

- thermoforming - a method using heat and a vacuum bed
- stereo copying - using a special swell paper which passes through a photocopier and then through a heating process to produce raised images.

Both methods are relatively easy but fairly expensive, especially stereo copying.

Making a tactile diagram. ▶

If a diagram is only to be used once then it is probably easier to use a collage approach. Be careful, however, not to spend time on making a diagram only to find the child really cannot understand it. Teaching the child to understand diagrams has to be included in curricular activities and will not occur incidentally.

For children with some remaining sight the combination of texture and colour is useful so children can back up remaining vision with touch, but colour confusion may be a feature of the child's eye condition so colour must be chosen carefully.

Listening skills

All children need to develop effective listening skills, for visually impaired children these skills are fundamental to their ability to gather, organise, retain, understand and utilise information. Unlike fully sighted children, visually impaired children cannot enhance auditory information with visual input.

The normal classroom environment tends to be quite noisy so visually impaired children must become adept at screening out superfluous sound and focusing on important sources of information. This has to happen from the early years in school as there are few noisier places than the average nursery.

It will be necessary for the classteacher to ensure that she helps by providing plenty of opportunities for the visually impaired child not only to identify sound sources but by emphasising the information she wants the class to pay particular attention to, using the names of the children first, to gain attention, before giving the information. This is especially important for the visually impaired child who will not necessarily know she is being spoken to.

How the teacher uses her voice is also important as the visually impaired child will need to be able to interpret changes in emphasis which indicate whether the teacher is praising her or is expressing dissatisfaction. If the child cannot see the teacher's face clearly she must therefore rely solely on these auditory prompts.

As children move on to more sophisticated levels of information gathering, their use of auditory information becomes more complex. Taped material offers a tremendous opportunity but children do need specific skills to be able fully to utilise recorded information.

Listening to the reading given by the talking thermometer. ▶

These would include:
- the development of sequential recall
- the ability to analyse and interpret information based on selective listening
- a sound understanding of word meaning and wide vocabulary
- the ability to organize recorded information.

There are many different ways for visually impaired people to use auditory materials. Tape is the most usual, but synthetic speech and human readers are also commonly used. Because of the sheer volume of material to be processed the child will need to learn how to use compressed speech. This means that auditory material can be played back at an accelerated speed to avoid 'real time' delays. The child will also need to be able to scan the recorded information to focus on the most important elements. The advent of easily portable tape players and the increasing use of car cassette systems by a sighted audience has widened the choice of taped materials as has the advent of compact discs. The old image of talking books for the blind being a very special facility has now given way to an accepted use of taped material by the general population.

Music
Many visually impaired children have an especial interest in music. Children who may experience considerable difficulties in many areas of academic work sometimes become accomplished musicians. Music also helps to refine existing listening skills as well as providing a creative approach to communication and self expression.

Some children can go on to learn braille music whilst others may require less orthodox approaches. Music should be available as part of the child's entitlement to the National Curriculum. If the child seems to be particularly involved and interested in music it may also be necessary to stipulate their need for music as part of their IEP and Statement.

Technology

The use of increasing amounts of technology by all children has lead to changes in teaching and expectations. For disabled people technology has brought greater access to the workplace and with it higher demands and expectations from employers. Those involved in supporting visually impaired children in mainstream or specialist provision will also be expected to become familiar and comfortable with a large range of both hardware and software equipment. Communication methods can now be as flexible as required, but children do need to be taught to develop skills which will make the technology available to them.

Touchtyping has always been a useful skill for visually impaired children and has become even more important with the increased use of 'qwerty' keyboards in word processing. As with other skill areas, visually impaired children should be taught systematically both to type and to use specific equipment. Teachers will need continually to update their own technology skills both by usage, training and research as new equipment comes on to the market.

Technology is not, however, a panacea. Careful assessment of the child and her curricular needs are essential. Technology is an expensive resource so we have to be clear why it is being used. Technology can be both a teaching aid as well as a tool for promoting access to the curriculum. The various aspects of its use overlap but teacher and child need to be aware of the purpose for which technology is currently being used and why the particular device chosen is considered especially appropriate.

Researching a history assignment using CD-ROM with speech. ▶

For support and teaching, technology can provide:
- help with the production of learning materials such as large print, braille, diagrams
- easy storage of potentially bulky material (such as braille)
- a means of sharing ideas and information with the child for later retrieval at home
- a network for information gathering
- an interactive medium for teaching specific skills.

For the child, access to technology can mean:
- more time available because less time has to be spent on mechanical operations
- a choice of methods of presentation and production
- more independence and control over learning
- auditory as well as hard copy retrieval
- a shared experience with fully sighted peers
- greater portability of material
- the development of 'saleable' skills
- stimulation of remaining vision and its more effective use
- access to research and reference materials.

There are some potential disadvantages:
- scarce resources spent on equipment rather than people
- equipment left unused in cupboards because of poor technical support and training
- technology being seen as 'the answer'
- unnecessary time wasted using technology when low-tech solutions would have been better
- children left alone to cope
- poor teaching hiding behind complex systems.

Devices available can be divided up into three sub groups:

- devices which use a visual output - these would include devices which can offer a choice of visual display to suit children with low vision.
- devices which produce an auditory output - this will help both blind and partially sighted users.
- devices which produce a tactile output (such as braille) - these devices would be used by educationally blind children.

Most devices will have a range of these outputs.

The method of input to systems may be:

- qwerty keyboard
- touch screen
- mouse
- concept keyboards
- switches
- sound
- optical character recognition (OCR)

Technology does intimidate some teachers. The provision of training both for staff and pupils will reduce anxieties but staff should be able to have access to ongoing support so that equipment is maintained and upgraded.

CHAPTER 5
TRAINING FOR INDEPENDENCE

One of the areas of specialist support which still holds a mystique is mobility training. Very few people, including parents of visually impaired children, really know what is meant by the terms 'mobility' and 'orientation'. Mobility in the context of visual impairment simply means the ability to travel independently. This might be travel to the local shops, around the school or a journey to work of several miles involving public transport.

The most famous mobility aid is the white cane, which in itself has become a symbol of blindness but in reality it is more a sign of independence. The other classic concept of blindness is the blind person as guide dog owner. The guide dog is another form of mobility aid. But being mobile would be of little value if the individual could not orientate themselves in the environment. They must know where they are and how to find their way to the next place they want to reach.

Mobility and orientation are vital independence skills and are needed from the very early years. Formal mobility training is carried out by a rehabilitation worker or mobility officer. These workers are employed either by Social Services, education support services or voluntary organisations. There are also freelance mobility consultants. Because mobility and orientation instructors are usually also rehabilitation workers they can also offer training in general independence skills. Mobility instruction can also involve other professionals such as physiotherapists or occupational therapists.

Mobility and orientation are vital independence skills. ▶

Mobility training in school

Mobility training as part of the curriculum for visually impaired children imposes some logistical difficulties. How can sufficient time be found in the school day? Are there conflicting and competing demands from other curricular areas? Would it not be better taught outside school hours? The answers to these questions will depend on the mobility requirements of the individual child.

At a basic level the child will want:

- to find her way around the classroom
- to move confidently, safely and independently around the school
- to be able to join peers in playground activities
- to take part in physical education
- to travel home independently
- to accept and efficiently use a sighted guide

Not all the child's mobility needs have to rely on a mobility instructor. Such instructors are unfortunately few and far between. Teachers and assistants have to play their part in the teaching of some basic skills and routes. Time has to be allowed during the school day for the child to be able to finish tasks independently and to move from one area to another. Without the ability to move easily and independently in a variety of different areas and locations the child will only ever have limited access to the curriculum. For this reason all severely visually impaired children should have mobility training and assessment included in their statement of special educational need.

Formal training will include these elements:
- assessment of mobility and orientation needs
- the use of low vision and auditory skills
- sighted guide technique
- how to be able to learn and plan routes
- the use of a range of different aids to mobility

Orientation training will concentrate on:
- sensory skill development
- the development of body image
- strategies and methods for walking in alignment (hand trailing, use of echolocation etc.), changing direction (turning)
- effective and systematic search and exploration
- the development of skills in judging distance, size and time
- navigation within the environment (obstacle detection and avoidance)

How and where this training is carried out will depend on the age and functioning of the child. Mobility not only comprises formal training, but is embedded in the child's attitude and motivation to be independent. Parents and teachers often have mixed feelings about this. In the early years our expectations will obviously be different from later ones but we must be prepared to 'let go' even if the child's mobility involves an element of risk and may include the odd bump and bang.

At a recent meeting a group of parents and teachers discussed mobility training, some of their comments were:

"But my child has no mobility problems."

"We expect too much from our children."

"But she's too young to do that on her own."

"Everyone needs a bit of help."

"I don't think he should be out after dark."

"It's nice that the other children always lend a hand."

"She always waits for Miss Brown to take her to the playground."

"He prefers sitting and chatting on a bench."

Parents of very young children quite often do not see their child as having mobility problems. What is hard for them to realize is that their child may need additional help for future skills and for the refinement of existing ones and that this may not develop automatically. We naturally want to protect children who seem especially vulnerable. Over-protectiveness is one of the issues which must be faced not only by parents but by all staff in mainstream schools.

It is worth noting that a severe visual impairment alone is not the cause of movement difficulties but produces problems linked to:
- **Poor motivation:** the child may gain little reward from movement or may have restricted opportunity to move independently.
- **Transitional movement:** the child feels stable in some positions and may be reluctant to adopt postural change.
- **Poor body awareness:** especially centre body awareness.
- **Spatial relations:** front/back; up/down; on/under; left/right discrimination.
- **A possible delay in the formation of basic concepts.**
- **Poor sensori motor integration:** sensory motor integration is the role the central nervous system plays in co-ordinating input from the sensory nerves. This is particularly important for the child's awareness of their movement and position as well as the development of good balance.
- **Fear.**

When assessing a child, general consideration should be given to:
- current visual functioning
- motor development and movement skills
- the child's level of concept formation
- the child's overall environmental awareness
- the child as a member of the family
- what the child feels are important skills (being able to get to the local chip shop or meet a friend for instance).

Visual skills will be particularly concerned with:
- localizing objects
- focusing on a moving object at a constant distance
- following the movement of an object towards and away.

Intervention will need to address problems linked to:
- erratic movement because of concentration on the immediate environment
- problems in crowded areas where visual confusion may inhibit confident movement
- unreliable edge detection including difficulties with surface and level variations
- limited ability to use vision to identify route landmarks
- uncertainty in dealing with road junctions and crossings
- poor visual adjustment to changing light conditions and possible night blindness.

Basic techniques for moving around school

Since many of the child's mobility and orientation skills will be needed in the school environment, teachers can play a major part in ensuring the child feels confident and secure. To offer specific help it is useful to know how to introduce the child to some basic movement techniques.

Sighted guide technique
Encourage the child to hold your arm above the elbow (or your wrist if she cannot reach your arm). The child will then be walking about half a pace behind you. When you wish to move in a restricted space (for example at the end of lessons when there are lots of other children in the corridor), just move your arm behind you. You will

The correct way for a young child to move with a sighted guide. ▶

63

then be walking in single file as the child will naturally move behind you.

When introducing the child to an unknown part of the school it is important to warn her of any steps and whether they are up or down. You don't need to count them as the child will feel from the movement of your arm when the steps end. With a young child you might want to count the steps as part of a game.

Finding a seat
Once children are familiar with the layout of their classroom they should be able to find their own seat, but in another room or in the hall you might need to assist them. It is best to place the child's hand on the back of the seat or to guide the child forward until her legs brush the front of the seat.

Building confidence
Never leave a severely visually impaired child alone in an empty room without giving them physical contact with a known wall area or piece of furniture.

In any new surroundings explain to the child what is around them but be sure to use descriptions you know they understand.

Remember, much language is visually loaded so try to call to a child so they can follow the sound of your voice rather than use too many explanatory terms.

Keeping safe
There will be many times in a school environment when a visually impaired child will want to explore independently. In order to develop this confidence the child can be taught to use her arm position to protect her body from too many bumps.

Using her arms to protect face and body while moving. ▶

The child should be taught to hold one arm at face level with the palm turning out and the elbow bent. The child's palm is in front of their face, thus any objects at head height hit the hand rather than the face.

The child's other arm is bent downwards and is kept about 12cms away from the body. This technique is useful for avoiding bumps below waist height.

Classroom familiarization

In a large secondary school there may be many changes of room for different subjects and even in a small primary school it can be surprising how many different areas may be used. The child will also have to find set locations such as toilet or dining areas. Remember that each time a child has changed classrooms it will be a different route to the same toilet!

An introduction to exploration within a room must use sound, light, olfactory and tactile clues. To find out how important this is just close your eyes and try to listen to the room. Where is the door or the window - are they open or closed? Is there a smell of food from the dining room? Are the toilets nearby (in most schools they smell quite strongly!)? Is there a sink in the room where the child may hear running water? What covering does the floor have?

To begin the exploration choose a fixed point. It might be the door or a large cupboard. It needs to be something easy to get to.

If the child you are working with has never had any mobility training then you will need to teach her to use her hands to trail. The child places her hand palm outwards on the surface to be explored. This is a safer hand position as fingers will naturally be pushed into the palm and away from the doorjamb. The child then gently moves her hand along the surface to be trailed. This gives the child security as well as information.

As the child locates furniture and fixtures in the room explain what they are and particularly notice windows, taps, switches and anything that may be strange to the child or may make a disturbing or surprising noise. In nurseries there are particularly noisy areas for play. In a secondary school there is electronic apparatus in science rooms which is visually unnoticeable but will buzz or click thus distracting the child. When the child has thoroughly explored the perimeters of the room she will need to explore the centre areas of the classroom methodically.

After exploring the room layout the child will need to make repeated trips to previously explored areas and objects which can become landmarks. For instance desk to door, door to desk, then desk to sink and sink to desk.

Routes around the school

By learning routes that can be followed independently the child develops confidence for later more ambitious routes. Like all the other skills learning a route requires a consistent approach to the language used in its description.

Landmarks and clues are best negotiated with the child. It is much more meaningful and therefore memorable if the child has pointed out a texture or sound that is part of the route than if a sighted helper takes all the responsibility for its construction. Study the timetable with the child and work out which are the most significant routes. Some will be easier than others. Don't try to do too much at once. Mobility requires enormous amounts of concentration by the child and too much information can confuse.

General principles of mobility training:

- tackle routes one at a time.
- walk through the route with the child and listen to what she says. You may need to point out that some things will not be in the same place every day and so cannot be used as landmarks. Explain any direction points where the child needs to turn.
- when you feel the child has got some idea of the route, let her try the easier bits with you walking behind but reassure her if and when necessary.
- when you feel the child is confident enough and you have discussed this with the child then let her go through the route with you following.
- go over the route together until you and the child are both satisfied she has mastered it.
- the child can then establish a series of routes that start from a known base.

Go over the route together until you are certain the child has mastered it. ▶

Effective searching

Independence is about responsibility and so looking after and organizing possessions is important. We all lose things and we all drop things onto the floor. This can be frustrating for any of us but to the visually impaired child learning to cope alone this can be especially upsetting.

There are some simple techniques which will help:

- help the child by presenting small objects in some kind of accessible container or tray. This will lessen the chance of objects dropping onto the floor.
- make sure the desk has adequate storage space.
- personal belongings will need to be secure but easily available.

If an object does drop:

- after the object has dropped the child will need to pause so she can locate the sound.
- the child will then need to move towards the sound. If the object is still very near they will have to bend or kneel on the floor and use circular sweeping hand movements radiating out until they locate the object. For young children this skill can be practised either by using a ball with a bell inside or by using a clock or other sound making device which can be placed on the floor and gradually moved further away. A child with low vision may be helped if training includes a very brightly coloured series of objects which can gradually be reduced in size.

Daily living skills

Working with parents of visually impaired children has continuing importance, but for a young visually impaired child the area of daily living skills is the focus for a real partnership between the child and their parents and teachers. Skills will take longer to develop and all those involved with the child will need to be active in this process. Daily living is where the child meets the outside world and all its expectations. Social skills are part of daily living and our consideration when working with the visually impaired child must relate to skill efficiency but also on how the child presents to others when performing a skill. This needs to be considered culturally, for example, eating with fingers rather than using a knife and fork may be accepted by some ethnic groups but not others.

Eating

Unless the child has other disabilities they should be feeding themselves independently by the time they reach school. They are likely to be using a spoon at the nursery stage but should be expected to master the use of implements just as the other children do. It is helpful in the early stages to use a non-slip mat and plateguard and to organise the food on the child's plate so they know where different textures and tastes appear. Eating with your eyes closed will soon indicate how unpleasant unexpected cold lettuce appears after a mouthful of hot food. Certain types of food such as peas and rice remain a challenge even to adult dexterity. Cutting meat is one of the harder skills to master and the smallest amount of residual vision helps enormously.

Learning to use a spoon and fork at nursery school. ▶

For children with low vision it is useful to:

- present food and drink from the side where the child has some vision.
- use plain coloured plates in light or very dark colours which contrast better against the food.
- use a mat which will provide contrast for cutlery.
- give the child time to cut up their own food or if limited time is available give them something they can eat independently.

When pouring:

- it is better and safer for a child to use a microwave for heating drinks than to pour boiling water.
- when pouring liquids the child can be taught to test the liquid level with their finger tip. Children with low vision will see the liquid level better if the inside of the cup is a plain colour.
- it is sometimes helpful to use a liquid level indicator (obtainable from the RNIB Resource Centre).

Dressing

Visually impaired children will vary tremendously in their self care skills.
Dressing at school will usually be:

- putting coats on
- getting ready for PE and games
- getting ready for swimming.

The most crucial aspect of dressing skills like so many other areas is to allow sufficient time for the child to dress themselves independently. Different teaching approaches may be used if a child has difficulty in a particular area. A skill area may need to be analyzed and taught very systematically. Generally there will be a need for children to have facilities so they can organize their belongings.

Socialisation

A severe visual impairment can isolate. Not only might the child be isolated by her disability but we can compound their isolation in our attempts to integrate and

support. The technology required by a visually impaired child can be substantial and quite logically some teachers will position the child in a corner where she can be surrounded by her equipment and support staff. A child's mobility needs may make the classteacher assume that the desk in the corner nearest the door is going to be easier for the child to manage. An over-keen support teacher or assistant may shadow the child throughout the school day. All our worthy efforts to help the child become 'integrated' may only make her more conscious of her isolation.

We should consider:
- how much time and what opportunities does the child have for privacy?
- does the child spend quality time with sighted peers?
- are ways found for common interests to be developed and shared?
- how much is the child asked for their opinion and do we act on their comments?
- are opportunities available for discussion with the class group?
- are the child's strengths known and valued?
- does the child have access to others with a similar disability?
- is responsibility shared amongst all the children including the visually impaired child?

The Code of Practice reminds us:

"Special educational provision will be most effective when those responsible take into account the ascertainable wishes of the child concerned..."

Independence has to be built on trust between children and adults. For visually impaired children this is particularly important.

Terms used in mobility training

Auditory: Related to or experienced through the sense of hearing.
Cane: There are three kinds of cane with a variety of different tips:
Symbol cane: A short white cane used to indicate the person carrying it has a visual difficulty.
Guide cane: A longer cane for users with some residual vision.
Long cane: A tool for independent travel used by functionally blind people. Longer than the other canes, it has a very specific technique for its use which needs to be taught by a specialist.
Clue: Any sound, smell, temperature, tactile or visual stimulus that helps to confirm position.
Direction point: A place which needs to be identified as it marks a change of direction or travel.
Landmark: Any familiar object, sound, smell, temperature or tactual clue that is easily recognised and that has a known location in the environment.
Route: The structure of landmarks and direction points to make it easier to learn to move over a distance of A to B.
Sound differentiation: The ability to distinguish between different useful sounds.
Sound localization: To determine the direction of a sound.
Tactual: Related to or experienced through the sense of touch.
Trailing: The act of using the fingers to follow a surface for any or some of the following:
- to determine one's position in space
- to locate specific objects
- to get a parallel line of travel.
Veering: A change in direction or course. Moving away from the desired line of travel.

References

Dodson-Burk, B., Hill, E.W., (1989), *An Orientation and Mobility Primer for Families and Young Children,* New York: American Foundation For The Blind

Dominguez,B., Dominguez,J., (1991), *Building Blocks: Foundations for Learning for Young Blind and Visually Impaired Children,* New York: American Foundation for the Blind

Dunlea, A., (1989), *Vision and the Emergence of Meaning, Blind and Sighted Children's Early Language,* Great Britain: Cambridge University Press

Fielder, A.R.,Best A.B.,Bax, C.O., (Eds), (1993), *The Management of Visual Impairment in Childhood,* London: MacKeith Press

Gardner, P.A., (1979), *ABC of Ophthalmology,* Articles From The British Medical Journal, England: British Medical Journal

Harrell, L., Akeson, N., (1987), *Preschool Vision Stimulation It's More Than a Flashlight!,* New York, American Foundation For The Blind

Hill, E., Ponder, P., (1976), *Orientation and Mobility Techniques: A Guide For The Practitioner,* New York, American Foundation For The Blind.

Jose, Randall T., (Ed), (1983), *Understanding Low Vision,* New York: American Foundation For The Blind

Osherson, D.N., Kosslyn, S.M., Hollerbach, J.M., (1990), *An Invitation To Cognitive Science, Visual Cognition And Action,* Volume 2, USA: The MIT Press

Pogrund, R.L.,Fazzi, D.L., Lampert, J.S., (Eds), (1992), *Early Focus,* New York: American Foundation For The Blind

Troster, H., Brambring, M., Beelman, A., (1990), *Stereotyped Behaviours in Blind Infants and Preschoolers,* University of Bielefeld: Project A3

Walker, E., Tobin, M., McKennell, A., (1992), *Blind and Partially Sighted Children in Britain: the RNIB Survey,* London: HMSO

Warren, D.H., (1984), *Blindness and Early Childhood Development,* New York: American Foundation For The Blind

Welsh, R.L., Blasch, B.B., (1980), *Foundations of Orientation and Mobility,* New York: American Foundation For The Blind

Sources of information and help

American Foundation for the Blind
15 West 16th Street
New York
NY10011
USA

Birmingham Royal Institution for the Blind
Queen Alexandra College
49 Court Oak Road
Harborne
Birmingham B17 9TG

ClearVision Project
Linden Lodge School
61 Princes Way
London SW19 6JB

Eye Care Information Bureau
4 Ching Court
Shelton Street
London WC2H 9DG

Guide Dogs for the Blind Association
Alexandra House
9/11 Park Street
Windsor
Berkshire SL4 1JR

LOOK
The National Federation of Families with Visually Impaired Children
Queen Alexandra College
49 Court Oak Road
Birmingham B17 9TG

Moorfields Eye Hospital
City Road
London EC1V 2PD

Royal National Institute for the Blind:

Education Information Service
RNIB Education & Leisure
224 Great Portland Street
London WIN 6AA

RNIB Education Centre London
Garrow House
190 Kensal Road
London W10 5BT

SENSE
13-15 Clifton Terrace
Finsbury Park
London

VIEW
Association for the Education and Welfare of the Visually Impaired
York House
Exhall Grange School
Wheelwright Lane
Ash Green
Coventry CV7 9HP